THE GHOST OF JOHNNY TAPIA

THE GHOST OF JOHNNY TAPIA

PAUL ZANON

with **TERESA TAPIA**

Foreword by **SAMMY HAGAR**

HAMILCAR NOIR

HARD-HITTING TRUE CRIME

ISBN: 978-1-949590-15-9

Publisher's Cataloging-in-Publication Data
Names: Zanon, Paul, author.
Title: The Ghost of Johnny Tapia / Paul Zanon.
Description: Boston, MA: Hamilcar Publications, 2019.
Identifiers: LCCN 2019944054 | ISBN 9781949590159
Subjects: LCSH Tapia, Johnny, 1967–2012. | Boxers (Sports)—United States—Biography. | BISAC SPORTS & RECREATION / Boxing. | BIOGRAPHY & AUTOBIOGRAPHY / Sports. | TRUE CRIME / General.
Classification: LCC GV1132.T36 Z36 2019 | DDC 796.83/092—dc23

Hamilcar Publications
An imprint of Hannibal Boxing Media
Ten Post Office Square, 8th Floor South
Boston, MA 02109
www.hamilcarpubs.com

Printed in the United States of America

On the cover: Johnny Tapia poses at a portrait session for Spin *magazine in 2000.*

Frontispiece: Johnny Tapia celebrates his victory over Manuel Medina after winning the IBF featherweight championship at The Theater at Madison Square Garden in New York City on April 27, 2002.

To the inspiration and legend, Johnny Lee Tapia.
Died before his time, but left a legacy
for several generations.

My father boxed at bantamweight, featherweight, and lightweight, fighting under a variety of names, including Bobby Hagar, Bobby Burns, and Cotton Burns. He was always taking fights at the last minute, getting in trouble for being drunk in the ring and getting banned. He needed the money and would change his name every time he went to a new town to get a fight. When he started he was really good and had a strong punch, but he kept going downhill because he was an alcoholic.

As for me, from as young as I can remember, my dad would call me "Champ" and introduce me as that, telling everyone I was going to be champion of the world. He had a little gym set up in the garage, and I boxed all over the neighborhood. I was pretty much thinking that was what I was going to do with my life, although I do remember seeing Elvis Presley on TV and watching my older teenage sisters going crazy over him and thinking, "Maybe I'm going to be that."

The turning point came when I was fifteen and a half. My dad took me to Los Angeles to the Main Street Gym, where Johnny Flores was training Jerry Quarry. We walked in and my dad said, "He's gonna be a fighter," and Johnny said, "Let's see what he can do." He put me in the ring with some Mexican guy, who'd had about thirty pro fights, and moments later this guy hit me. The moment it landed, I thought, "Man. I have never been hit like that in my life and I don't ever wanna be hit like that again!"

My dad had already applied for my professional boxing license and even lied about my age to get me the forms. After that sparring session, I went home and I was filling everything out, and my mom was crying as she watched. "You're not going to do that. You're not going to be like your father." I stopped and said, "You know what. You're right." My head was still ringing from that freakin' left hook I took from this Mexican dude. That was it. I don't think I ever put on a set of gloves again.

• • •

Roll the clock forward to the 1990s and I'm at a David Tua fight in Vegas. Johnny Tapia comes up to me and says, "Hey. Sammy Hagar. The Red Rocker! I'm Johnny Tapia." I replied, "I know exactly who you are!" Everybody knew who Johnny was. I then said, "Let's exchange numbers. It would be great to go to the fights together." We exchanged numbers and he'd call all the time. Even at 4 a.m. "Hey brother. What's happening? You ain't giving me no love. I ain't heard from you for like a week." He was always joking around, and you couldn't help but just love the guy.

Every time I'd meet with Johnny, there'd be a story to tell after. One time, I'm in Vegas, staying in a hotel and we're going to go to a fight together. I'm waiting in the lobby looking at my watch thinking, "Is he ever turning up?" About an hour later, his wife Teresa walks over and says, "We were here on time, but as Johnny was waiting in the lobby for you, some guy was giving the lady behind the desk some shit and Johnny went up to him and said, 'Hey man. Stop being rude to the lady,' and the guy said, 'Fuck you.' Johnny knocked the guy out in the lobby and his buddy took off running. Johnny took after him, then the cops arrived. So

Johnny was late because he was filling out papers for the cops." You had to love him for that.

Then in 2002, Johnny gave me the opportunity to do something I could have only dreamed of: working his corner. Not just any old corner though. I was alongside Freddie Roach, and Johnny was fighting the incredible Marco Antonio Barrera. When he asked me, I said, "Sure. But I don't know how to work a corner!" He said, "Don't worry about that, man." I asked Freddie Roach what to do and he said, "Yeah. Don't worry. You just put the stool in there. You're gonna be the stool guy. You put it through the ropes, right before he comes over at the end of each round." He gave me a little bit of coaching on how to do it and I thought, "Fuck it. Yeah. I'll work the corner."

The problem was, Johnny wanted me there as a motivation guy to give him a pep talk in between rounds, because I'm high energy. I go to the dressing room where they are warming up for the fight and Freddie takes me aside and says, "Listen. Nobody says anything in the corner but me. You understand?" and I say, "Sure." Johnny sees what's going on and loves winding Freddie up and says to me, "Sammy. When I'm in that corner, I need you to get me all pumped up." Freddie's looking at me shaking his head saying, "I do all the talking."

Johnny now starts his warm-up and is throwing his left hooks on the mitts. It was exhilarating to witness how fast and hard Johnny would throw those punches and how quick his feet were. I was like, "Holy shit." I've been in a few dressing rooms before but I'd never seen anybody warming up like that. All of a sudden, bang, he dislocates his shoulder. Completely pops out of the socket. I'm thinking, "This fight is over." Johnny moves his arm around, pops it back in. A minute later, it pops out again and Johnny once again pops it back in like it's a normal thing to do. I'm thinking, "This is crazy. I've never seen anything like this before." I was so nervous and scared for him.

We then walk out into the crowd, which was incredible. The fight starts, and every time he came back to the corner he kept saying, "Sammy baby. You ain't showing me no love, man. I ain't feeling the love Sammy!"

I'm looking at Freddie and then turned to Johnny a bit hesitant and said, "Go get him Johnny!" The truth is, I was thinking, "I really can't help this guy." When you listened to one of the best trainers in the world in Freddie Roach and what he was saying, I just didn't feel I belonged there. My band was sitting ringside right behind me and I kept looking at them saying, "Oh fuck!" It's different being in the corner. Everything looks different than when you're spectating as a fan.

Back in the early days, in 1974, I opened with Montrose for The Who at Wembley Stadium, London, in front of about eighty thousand people. That was less nerve-wracking than being in the corner for Johnny. I've got goose bumps on my arms just talking about it right now. What an experience and what a privilege to have shared that time with Johnny.

• • •

The last time I ever spoke with Johnny was in 2009, when he was in the hospital in a coma from one of his binges. Teresa would call and put me on the phone to him, to see if he'd wake up. They'd even brought in a priest who was reading him his last rights, basically saying, "Yup. This is it. He's not going to pull out of it this time." The doctors were ready to pull the plug, then about ten days into the coma, I'm chatting to him and he screamed, "I Can't Drive 55!" and he came out of his coma. That was the last time I spoke to Johnny, and that kind of summed up the man he was.

Johnny had incredible heart, was such a sweet man, but was also tormented. He had two sides to him. The sweetest, nicest guy, but then the other side that could probably kill you. He was tortured with his addictions, but Johnny was always pure emotion in that ring. In his heyday, with his speed and skill, he was one of the greatest bantamweight champs ever.

Sammy Hagar
San Francisco, California
January 2019

D.O.A.

*"The only difference between a genius and insanity,
is that insanity has no limits."*
—Albert Einstein

The first time I met Johnny was at a daytime barbeque, and two weeks later, here we were at Wells Park Community Center in Albuquerque getting married.

As soon as we said our vows, he turned to me and said, "Now you can never leave me."

Those were shocking words to me. "What do you mean?" I replied.

Straight after the ceremony, everyone left and headed to my mom's house for the party reception, which was news to me and my mom! Johnny and his friends, however, knew all about it and couldn't wait to get into the cases of beer.

We show up at my mom's house and I wasn't feeling well. I had a bad cold, felt feverish, had a cough and sore throat. I wasn't in the party spirit. All I wanted to do was relax, but instead I was sitting there watching Johnny run around with tons of people in the house. What I didn't realize was that Johnny had already been on a binge all week. Not an alcohol binge though.

Next thing, Johnny disappeared, and one of his friends said, "Do you know what you've married?"

"What do you mean?" I replied.

"Go to the bathroom and take a peek at what you've married."

I walked to the bathroom and when I opened the door, Johnny was in there with another guy, who had a needle in Johnny's arm. I was blown away. I had never, ever witnessed that kind of drug abuse. Johnny slammed the door on me and locked it, but I kicked it down. By this stage it was too late. He'd already shot up. I was shouting at him, "Oh my God! How could you do this? Why are you doing this?" He was oblivious though as he was now high. He just walked out of the bathroom, straight past me as if I wasn't there, and partied some more. I felt mad, betrayed, upset, disgusted, and devastated.

Before I could even let that shock set in, suddenly there were police everywhere. Johnny was fighting in the street against someone and the police were going to arrest him. My mom is the one who saved him. She explained that we'd just got married and that I'd be responsible for him. You have to remember that the police at this time were not fans of Johnny because he came with a bad reputation—one I wasn't fully acquainted with.

The police let Johnny go on the condition that he left the house straightaway. So we got our luggage, put it in the car, and told everyone goodbye. Johnny was upset, as he didn't want to leave the party. The police made me drive as he sat next to me in the passenger seat, high and drunk. When we got a few blocks away, he had me stop the car, jumped over, and got into the driver's seat.

Friends of the family had given Johnny and me a really nice suite for our honeymoon at one of the best hotels in The Heights, which would normally go for a thousand dollars a night. I noticed we weren't going in the direction of the hotel and asked, "What are you doing? Where are we going?"

Johnny said, "I don't want to go there." Instead, he drove us to this dumpy fleabag motel called "The French Quarters," which was known for drug use and prostitution.

We got there, walked through the door, and in under a couple of minutes he said, "I need to make a phone call."

"There's a phone right here in the room," I replied.

"No, I need to use a pay phone," Johnny said. "I'll be right back."

What I didn't realize was that he took my car keys and the wedding money, which was approximately $500. No Johnny, no car, and no money. I was ashamed and embarrassed. I didn't know what to say to people and felt very alone. I was sitting in that room thinking, "What the hell am I going to do now?"

I called my mom just so someone knew where I was. "Change of plans, mom. We didn't go to the Sheraton hotel, we're at this motel." She asked why. "Oh. It was closer," I lied. I was too embarrassed to explain. I spent that night alone, scared, and put furniture up against the hotel room door.

The next morning, before 7 a.m., there's banging at the door and I thought, "It's Johnny!" I ran to the door and opened it, but it was my mom standing there crying.

"What's wrong?" I asked.

She wouldn't stop hugging me and kept saying, "Thank God you're OK."

I asked again, "What's wrong?"

She had her car parked outside and said, "Get your stuff. We've gotta go."

"Where are we going?" I asked.

"The hospital."

"Why?"

"Somebody called. Johnny's passed away. They found him dead in your car and was pronounced DOA [dead on arrival] at a fire station in the South Valley. He was then taken to UNM [University of New Mexico] hospital. You need to go to identify his body."

As we walked into the hospital, my head was all over the place. All of a sudden I heard screaming and yelling, and in a flash I saw Johnny run right past me. I was looking at him in this hospital gown, and his butt

3

cheeks were showing because he didn't have underwear on. He didn't even notice me as he ran past, and I looked at my mom and said, "Is this a sick joke?" In the meantime, hospital staff, security, and police were chasing Johnny. I was standing there with my mouth open.

My mom and I left, and as we were driving up a busy road I saw somebody running. It was Johnny. We pulled over beside him and he jumped in the car and said, like we've just done a bank job, "Let's go, let's go!" We drove to my grandma's house and as soon as we got in, he fell asleep like the dead for two days.

That was my first twenty-four hours as Mrs. Johnny Tapia.

Teresa Tapia

Baptism of Hell

*"Life doesn't run away from nobody.
Life runs at people."*
—Joe Frazier

Albuquerque, New Mexico, is geographically situated in a bygone era of gunslingers and fast drinkers. The Wild West, from 1865 to 1895, ingrained itself in America's folklore, and when John Lee Tapia was born there on February 13, 1967, it's as if he picked up the baton, ran with it, and left a trail of smoke behind him that immortalized *Mi Vida Loca.*

Was Johnny Tapia boxing's most tortured soul? Arguably. Known by boxing aficionados as a colorful multiweight world champion, Johnny stared death in the face more times than would seem physically possible.

As a seven-year-old boy, he was given his first taste of how quickly the circle of life can end for an individual at any given moment. While on a bus as part of a school field trip, Johnny was sitting next to a woman named Concha, who was heavily pregnant. The bus hit a rock while going down a mountain road, went off a cliff, and Johnny flew straight down the bus and cracked his head open, lying there barely conscious. Concha was also propelled out of her seat, through the bus window, but was then jammed between the bus and the tree. Her blood was literally dripping on Johnny as she died in front of his eyes.

This, however, was not the episode that would affect Johnny's mental health for the rest of his life. The day his mother Virginia gave birth to him, he was already absorbing second-degree shock: His father was murdered when his mother was pregnant with him. But it was a horrific episode that took place eight years later that was the beginning of the end for Albuquerque's most decorated boxer and New Mexico's most infamous athlete.

On May 24, 1975, an uncharacteristically tearful Johnny was taken to his grandparents' house while his mother was looking forward to going out dancing. He described her as wearing dark blue slacks and a beautiful white blouse. She was the most important person in his life, the human being he owed everything to. His best friend, his parent, the person who loved him, encouraged him, dressed and fed him.

Johnny pleaded with her not to go, claiming he had a bad feeling he couldn't explain. Something in the pit of his stomach wanted to be with her, protect her, and under no circumstances did he want her to go dancing. His mother had been on the sore end of a violent relationship a couple of years before, during which Johnny had intervened with a steak knife, stabbing the boyfriend to defend her. He was only five. His intervention worked on that occasion, and perhaps he sensed that air of vulnerability again.

Unable to fight back his tears, Johnny begged his grandparents to let him go to the dance. At this point, his mother handed him a Snickers bar as a treat, which acted as the necessary calming tool. From that day forth, before every fight, amateur and professional, he had to have a Snickers bar. As Johnny took the candy, his mother kissed him and said, "I'll be back tomorrow." She then headed off.

Despite the short-term comfort of the candy, Johnny, unable to sleep, remained an emotional wreck and spent the whole night looking frantically out the windows, waiting for his mother to return. He kept telling his grandparents, "I want my mom, I want my mom," but he was unloading on deaf ears.

Then came that haunting memory: the last time he would see his mother alive. Looking out of the back porch in the middle of the night, Johnny saw a pickup truck with two men riding up front and a woman tied up inside it. He was even convinced that his mother locked a frightened stare with him for a split second. He immediately went and woke up his grandparents, describing vividly what he'd just witnessed, right down to the color and type of truck (which would later match police reports). His grandparents dismissed his cries for help and instead punished the little boy for waking them up. Johnny's mother never did come home.

Soon after Johnny spotted the truck, his mother was driven to a remote gravel pit in the Southwest Valley of Albuquerque.

Johnny's interpretation of the attack as a little boy was that she was tied up and stabbed twenty-seven times with an ice pick, but the coroner's reports would confirm it was actually a screwdriver and an open pair of scissors. It was such a brutal attack that one of her breasts was almost completely severed.

Somehow she managed to crawl out of the pit, and when nearby workers found her, it looked like she had been aiming to crawl to the local houses in the distance. They called the police instantly and described her as wearing a red blouse—her white shirt was no longer recognizable amid the blood-drenched scene.

As the days went by, Johnny kept asking his grandparents what was going on. Nobody from his family called the police, but three days after he'd last seen her, Johnny was in the living room when there was a knock at the door. It was a family member holding a newspaper, showing an article to Johnny's grandparents about an unidentified woman wearing unique jewelry. The woman had been found brutally attacked and was in intensive care. The family member said, "Isn't this Virginia's jewelry?" The grandparents confirmed, "That's hers," then rushed down to the hospital without Johnny.

Virginia was in a coma, hanging onto life from a thread, but nonetheless still alive. She then received one last visit that ensured her fate: A man, believed to be one of her assailants, walked in with a blunt object and struck her across the head. Virginia Gallegos died in the hospital on May 28, 1975, four days after saying goodbye to her beloved son. Johnny later said his mother's death would "kill" him every day he remained on this planet.

Understandably, Johnny was left emotionally scarred. Irreparably, to be more accurate. In the coming years he refused to go to her grave and on one of the rare occasions he did muster the strength to see her resting site, he tried to take his life. He threw himself on top of a large knife, but somehow only the tip penetrated. Johnny took that as a sign that it was not his time.

This would not be his only tango with death.

Meeting His Match

*"If someone had said to me at the age of nineteen,
'Hey Teresa. What interest do you have in the
115-pound division?' I probably would have thought
they were joking and said, 'Do people even
fight at that kind of a weight?'"*
—Teresa Tapia

Turning to boxing at the age of nine, Johnny had a very impressive amateur career, becoming a two-weight national Golden Gloves champion. Happy with what he'd achieved, he threw his hat into the professional boxing ring on March 28, 1988.

With his relentless come-forward style and often lighthearted presence, he quickly became recognized by the media as a crowd pleaser, an entertainer. Having won the USBA super-flyweight title on May 10, 1990, against Roland Gomez, which he went on to defend four times in the next five months, Johnny boasted an unbeaten record of twenty-one victories and one draw and was being lined up for a world-title shot and a million-dollar Pepsi commercial.

Unfortunately, his passion and desire in the ring played second fiddle to a destructive lifestyle, one that a twenty-year-old Teresa Chavez, now Tapia, witnessed in horror hours after being married.

Johnny hadn't divulged much of himself to Teresa prior to getting hitched. He had gang connections, had been in and out of jail, and was facing prison time for intimidating a witness in a murder trial. That last action was the reason his professional boxing license had been suspended.

Without the strict discipline of professional prizefighting, Johnny was a lost soul, drinking and drugging himself into oblivion.

He was pronounced DOA on five occasions. "Five times that I know of—or, should I say, that I was aware of when he was with me," says Teresa. The first time was on the day of their wedding and the second was in the fall of 1993, when he'd been found in the streets of Albuquerque with a stab wound in his head, having also overdosed on narcotics.

Brushing off his second encounter with death, on December 23, 1993, fresh out of a three-month jail stint for breaking his probation conditions for driving under the influence of alcohol, Johnny came home, promising Teresa he was a changed man. They had recently lost a baby, four months into pregnancy, and he knew she was fed up with his antics. So he was on his best behavior, for a number of hours at least. On Christmas Eve, Johnny decided to visit his grandparents and promised he'd be back soon.

As Teresa waited in their tiny one-bedroom apartment, angry and disappointed, she hatched a plan to contain the unruly Johnny. In his absence, she had wrought-iron bars fitted on all the windows and door, then simply waited for his inevitable return.

One week later, on New Year's Day, Johnny waltzed back in after a weeklong drug binge. He was expecting a verbal shakedown from Teresa, but instead she hit him with a smile and said, "Get some rest." He went to sleep thinking he'd got the upper hand on his wife, but instead he'd awoken the devil in her. The moment he fell asleep, she cut a piece of carpet and hid the only key to the solitary door of their apartment underneath. She also had the phone disconnected while he was sleeping. In essence, she was taking away his contact with the outside world, which was his route to refuel with drugs and alcohol.

Johnny slept soundly for three days, and when he awoke Teresa fed him a huge meal. As he ate his food, she informed him that he was locked in and would not be leaving until he was clean. Naturally, this update from Teresa didn't go over too well. Johnny instantly became angry, began threatening her, tried getting out, and attempted to make a phone call.

Within a couple of days, Johnny began displaying withdrawal symptoms, shaking, vomiting, and complaining that his body was aching. He begged Teresa to unlock the door, but she stuck to her guns, sat in a chair calmly, and read a book to pass the time, which incensed him further. As a fighter with an all-action style, Johnny thrived off being hit. That first punch in his face was the necessary trigger to engage him in battle. Teresa, however, was not participating in any physical or verbal exchanges, and for the first time in their marriage, she was in complete control.

Teresa's mother would bring food and slip it through the bars, but she wouldn't be allowed to enter the property, as Teresa didn't trust anyone who might feel sorry for Johnny and potentially help him escape. The calmer Teresa acted, the more unnerved Johnny became. He started pacing up and down like a caged tiger, tore up the books she was reading in front of her, started yelling a tirade of obscenities, and smashed anything within reach. Despite putting herself in physical danger, and no matter what Johnny did, Teresa refused to let him break her. She did admit, however, that "the first couple of weeks, it felt like I was living in the movie *The Exorcist*. Things were bad."

By the third week, Johnny turned a corner. Despite still being extremely agitated and angry, he started doing push-ups and sit-ups, which made Teresa think, "OK. This is different behavior." By the fourth week, he was working out as much as he could, but, more important, with the clearest head he'd had on his shoulders for a very long time.

Incredibly, Teresa had no idea about Johnny the boxer. When they got married in 1992, Johnny was a guy she was married to who got into a lot of street fights and had a criminal reputation. She'd never once seen him box, and it's not something he talked about actively. So when he started training in the house, she had no idea that Johnny had a goal in mind: to return to professional boxing.

It wasn't until after the fifth week when he started talking to her about his career and she asked "Boxing? When? Why?" that Johnny replied, "That's what I did. Boxing is all I know. I was actually very good at it."

He then stopped and said, "I have a manager, you know?"

Teresa was even more bemused now. "Manager? Someone has managed you?"

"Yeah. My manager and trainer, Paul Chavez."

Within a couple of weeks, Teresa made the bold move to unlock the door and call Chavez. Aware of the situation, Chavez devised a routine that would only allow Johnny to drift between training and his apartment. Chavez told Teresa, "You have him ready at 5 a.m. We will go for a run, then go to training and I'll take him back to you at 5 p.m., and you lock him in." That became the routine.

In a matter of days, Chavez was on the phone to Top Rank, organizing Johnny's comeback fight against Jaime Olvera on the undercard of Tommy Morrison versus Brian Scott, at the Expo Square Pavilion, Tulsa. The date was March 27, 1994, almost six years to the day from his debut.

But could a twenty-seven-year-old Johnny regain his previous form after such a berserk three and a half years since last stepping through the ropes?

Escape to Victory

*"What made Johnny Tapia a great fighter?
Being Johnny Tapia. He trained hard and brought
entertainment with him. When he put all that
together in the ring, doing all that funny stuff,
he was unbeatable."*
—Eddie Mustafa Muhammad

Through an innate animal instinct to win, Johnny disposed of Olvera in four rounds on March 27, 1994. Teresa, who had been crying throughout the whole fight as Johnny exchanged blows, ran over to him straight after the fight was over and said, "You don't need to do this anymore. I'll go back to work."

"That's what I do," he replied. "This is where I feel at home. At peace."

Johnny went on to rack up four more wins in four months, the last of the quartet against Oscar Aguilar for the NABF super-flyweight title on July 15, 1994, knocking him out in three rounds. He had now earned the right to fight for the vacant WBO world super-flyweight title against El Salvador's Henry Martinez—a height not yet reached and a goal seemingly unthinkable only a few months before.

To think that Johnny had put his demons behind him and that he was sober going into the Martinez fight would be foolish. Straight after the Aguilar fight, he was sucked back into the drug-infested gutter he'd only just pulled himself out of. In the words of Teresa, "It was a very delicate time."

Fully aware of all the love and affection from the media and general public Johnny had received since his return, Teresa had to take him out of town soon after the fight when he got arrested for trying to sell imitation drugs to a police officer. The highs in the ring were contrasted with the comments Teresa would have to digest outside. "You're married to that drug-user gangbanger!" people would shout. She had entered into a new world, one that she had to adapt to very quickly.

The venue for Johnny's first world-title shot was "The Pit" in Albuquerque. There's something about the word "pit" that summons images of brutality, unfortunate connotations of large dogs fighting in fenced-off areas with people betting money to see a victim get carried away. Closer to home, Johnny's mother was murdered in a pit. Also, a pit is, in essence, a large hole in the ground; and on October 12, 1994, onlookers from the seats above him, in almost gladiatorial fashion, looked down at their homeboy flying the flag for Albuquerque.

Johnny stopped Martinez in the eleventh round to clinch his first world title. He had snatched an unlikely victory in the face of defeat, even though he was confidently ahead on the scorecards. Defeat appearing in the form of addiction, homelessness, street fighting, and close to a four-year enforced hiatus from boxing. Beating Martinez signaled Johnny's rebirth in the professional ranks, against all odds.

Johnny did his trademark backflip, but landed flat on the canvas intentionally, laying there watching the ceiling almost in disbelief at his incredible achievement. When he rose, he tearfully dedicated the win to his mother and grandparents.

Two fights later and Johnny was defending his title against Argentinian Jose Rafael Sosa on February 10, 1995. Adding muscle in Johnny's corner for this particular fight was someone better known for trading blows on screen. When interviewed on the night of the fight as to the merits of his presence, Mr. T replied, in a voice reminiscent of "Clubber" Lang from *Rocky III*, "I worked in the corner with him in May 1994. I've been in corners before, so I know what I'm doing. I'm not going to be fumbling around like a load of makeup guys in Hollywood. I know what I'm doing."

The list of celebrities over the years to work Johnny's corner alongside his trainers became impressively extensive, including Mickey Rooney, Mickey Rourke, Darius McCrary, William Forsythe, and Sammy Hagar. Rooney had a particularly profound effect on Johnny. The legendary actor played a boxer in the film *Killer McCoy*, and like Johnny was full of energy and a fast talker. He spent a lot of time with Johnny over the years, and when Johnny would pray in the dressing room, there would often be pictures of Rooney standing with his hand on Johnny's shoulder, praying with him. Often referred to by the media as Johnny's surrogate father, Rooney acted as a sounding board and source of wisdom. On one occasion, Johnny was upset because the media was bothering him.

"What's wrong, Johnny?" Rooney asked.

"The media. Doesn't matter what I do, they always knock me," Johnny told him.

"Is that all that's bothering you?" Rooney told him. "Let me tell you something. Sit down right here." Johnny sat down and listened intently.

Rooney continued. "Are they spelling your name right when they're talking about you?"

"Probably, I guess."

"Well don't worry about it then. When they stop writing about you, that's when you gotta worry! Take it from me."

With the content and color from his life, one thing was certain: the media would always be interested in the latest installment from Johnny Tapia.

• • •

On May 6, 1995, Johnny made his second title defense against Ricardo Vargas at Caesars Palace, Las Vegas. Despite one judge giving Johnny the nod against Vargas, two judges ruled it a draw after the fight was stopped in round eight on a technicality, due to a bad cut over Vargas's left eye from an accidental clash of heads. The weather on the day was well over one hundred degrees, and when Johnny stepped out of the ring, he fainted from exhaustion and was taken to the hospital.

Not one to hang around, Johnny had his next fight lined up eight weeks later. He would be taking on Arthur Johnson on July 2, 1995, an adversary he'd beaten already in the amateurs. By now, however, it was evident that Johnny's biggest fights were out of the ring, and very few weeks went by without some kind of jaw-dropping story.

A few weeks into the Johnson training camp, Teresa received a call saying that her brother Robert, who Johnny was very close to, had tried to commit suicide via an overdose. They rushed to the hospital and spent three days in the intensive care unit not knowing whether Robert was going to make it. On the third day, Johnny decided to go home so he could rest and begin training in the morning.

A few hours after he left the hospital, news came that Robert was out of danger and was going to pull through. An exhausted Teresa decided to rush home and surprise Johnny, but he was nowhere to be found. She tried to keep the faith initially, telling herself that maybe he'd just gone out for a jog. After trying to call him on his cell phone a number of times, she decided to get some rest on the couch.

Around 4:30 a.m., she was awoken by banging on the door. It was Johnny, high on some type of hallucinogenic. Teresa tried reasoning with him, but he was on another planet, so she decided to pack a bag and headed to her mother's house. As she was trying to leave, Johnny ran after her, waving a loaded gun at her yelling, "I'm going to kill you, then I'm going to kill myself." The strength of the drugs was overwhelming, and half the time he didn't know who Teresa was. He kept calling her different names of guys, saying things like, "You think I forgot? I'm going to shoot you and then I'm going to take them all out."

Teresa tried to calm him down but nothing was working, so she threatened to call 911. Instead, Johnny ran in the house and dialed the number himself. She ran up behind him and hung up the phone, but the operator called back immediately and informed her that help was on the way.

Teresa told Johnny that the cops would be there any minute, so he emptied the gun of bullets and took off. Minutes later, the trailer-park community where they lived was surrounded by police with dogs as well as by helicopters and news crews. In the meantime, Johnny had taken refuge under a truck and had covered himself from head to toe in motor oil to put the dogs off his scent. It worked.

A few hours later, the police left and Johnny surfaced. A flabbergasted Teresa looked at him and could only come up with, "You need to take a shower." To make matters worse, Top Rank was flying in that morning for a press conference with Johnny and Arthur Johnson to promote the upcoming fight. After he was done showering, Teresa went in to take a shower herself, giving Johnny strict instructions not to open the door or answer the phone no matter what. As soon as she jumped in the shower, she could hear Johnny talking. Teresa immediately got dressed and couldn't believe her eyes: Johnny had allowed the media to come in.

High as hell, there he was in front of the media as they filmed him addressing a number of invisible people and petting his nonexistent dogs. Because Johnny had invited them in, the media refused to leave, so Teresa had their attorney rush over to defuse the situation. Top Rank held the press conference without Johnny, with the police present in healthy numbers as there was now a warrant out for Johnny's arrest for the gun incident. In the meantime, Teresa and Johnny skipped town for a few days until things calmed down.

• • •

Despite a chaotic training camp, Johnny still managed to fight and beat Arthur Johnson, taking a majority decision in a very close fight. It wasn't an easy ride, however. Johnson had beaten Johnny in the amateurs and still possessed lightning hand speed and good power.

The contest was aired live on ABC's *Wide World of Sports* and was viewed by millions worldwide, with the pair willing to leave it all in the ring on fight night. Johnny hit the canvas twice, with one instance being recorded as a knockdown in the final round. One judge scored it a draw and the other two had Johnny winning by a small margin. Johnny won, but it wasn't a definitive victory.

That same night, armed with a cashier's check for $66,000, Johnny disappeared again. This was, to an extent, regular behavior for him. There were times right after his fights that he would have people leave drugs in his dressing room so he could start his binge. The binge could go on for one or two weeks, but also for three or four months.

"You could never gauge it. There was no pattern to figure out," Teresa recalls. "Trust me, I tried. In twenty years I couldn't figure it out. Literally, the weather could trigger him. I used to get mad at him and say, 'Why can't me and the kids be enough for you?'"

Johnny had two mistresses: One was Teresa, the other was drugs. Whenever she was with him, she knew she could keep him from going too crazy, but the thing was, she couldn't be with him every single second. The problem was, the drugs could.

Johnny had to be in court in eight days for the gun offense, and failing to do so would guarantee him a warrant and an eighteen-month jail sentence. Despite this being a post-fight norm for Johnny, Teresa was worried sick. Being married to an addict is possibly the hardest and most unstable job in the world.

As a wife, Teresa wanted the best for him, but realistically, there was never a "best." As a boxing manager, she was negotiating multimillion-dollar paydays for him, yet half the time she didn't even know where he was or whether he was going to make the fight or end up in prison, in the news, or in a hospital. And when he did hit the media for being in trouble for drugs, Teresa would downplay it and put him into a mental health facility, claiming he was having a bout of depression or some other mental disorder, because he wouldn't get judged so harshly for that.

Remedies to break the cycle included moving locations and getting help from counselors, rehab centers, and churches. But everything was cosmetic. No definitive solutions were ever found. This time, Teresa decided to hatch a resourceful plan to track down and kidnap Johnny. Confident that she would locate him, Teresa had her mother, stepfather, brother, and a number of others at their house assigned with the task of blocking the exits on his return.

After searching in some of Albuquerque's toughest hangouts, she suddenly remembered an old warehouse on 2nd Street, which was notoriously dangerous and crammed with drug dealers. Johnny would often tell her, "Never go there without me," but Teresa was desperate and particularly worried about making it to court on time.

That Friday, three days from the court date, Teresa went to the warehouse. She planned to go in at about 1:30 a.m. flanked by a friend and male cousin and play it off like they were just walking into a bar, looking for a drink. Her friend and cousin smoked cigarettes, which Teresa hated, especially in the car, but on that night she let them: she wanted to smell like she'd been in a bar. They'd also packed a few wine coolers, which they opened just as they pulled up and took a few swigs so they'd also smell of alcohol.

They knocked on the door, and the immediate reaction from the man who answered was, "He's not here."

"I didn't come to see Johnny," Teresa replied. "We just got done at a bar and we're looking for a place to go."

The man looked at them, saw two girls and said with a smile, "Well come in then!" In walked Teresa, for the first time in her life.

Moments after she sat down, the men next to her started passing drugs around. Teresa, confident yet petrified, said, "Oh, no thank you, we had some earlier," not realizing that these men didn't stop after one hit. Then they offered liquor, but Teresa was scared to drink it, thinking it might be laced with drugs.

Less than ten minutes after Teresa arrived, Johnny appeared. He steamed over to Teresa like a bull, grabbing her by the arm and hair. His friends who were flirting with her said, "Leave her alone, Johnny. She's having fun."

"That's my wife!" he snapped. He dragged her outside to take her home, thinking he was in charge, but little did he know that he'd just landed firmly in Teresa's web. He had no idea what was about to happen.

When they arrived back home and Johnny saw a house full of people, he tried to run off. When that failed, he had a huge argument with Teresa, but eventually calmed down. Teresa had a doctor check Johnny out and give him a drug test to see what was in his system. (The doctor was about to administer prescription drugs and didn't want Johnny to experience an adverse reaction.) The doctor then knocked Johnny out with what was known as a "kick it" kit (a common practice in most rehab centers), which would help him rest but also help wean him off the drugs.

The concoction kept Johnny asleep until Monday, and he made it to the courtroom and through the process without any battles. When he walked out of court, because he was so out of it, Johnny had no idea that he'd agreed to be thrown out of New Mexico for eighteen months.

The moment he got home, he was administered another dose of drugs by the doctor to keep him sedated, then Teresa, her mother, stepfather, and brother drove up to Big Bear, California, where Oscar De La Hoya had set up a lovely house for them. The faster option was to fly, but the instability of Johnny on a plane frightened everyone, so they opted for the eight-hundred-mile, twelve-hour drive. Soon after arriving at Big Bear, everyone but Teresa left, and the drugs soon wore off. The first night Johnny woke up, he fell down the stairs and was screaming, "Treesa, Tree. I'm tripping. I'm tripping bad." The house they had in Albuquerque didn't have any stairs, so he was convinced he was in the middle of a bad hallucinogenic episode.

Johnny continued, "I can't get out of this. I'm still tripping. I don't know what I took and don't know where I'm at. Help me."

Before Teresa could explain anything, he ran outside, looked around, and said, "Where am I? I can't get off this trip. Wow. Whatever I took was strong. What did I take?"

"Calm down, Johnny," Teresa told him. "We're in Big Bear. You were thrown out of New Mexico as part of your agreement in court, which you agreed to. This is our new home."

An incensed Johnny threatened to run away saying, "I don't want to live here. I don't care what you say. I'm going home."

A composed Teresa replied, "Go ahead. Run away. We're at the top of a mountain. You'll either get lost or exhausted."

Oscar De La Hoya and his trainers kept waiting at the gym for Johnny, but he refused to go. It wasn't until Teresa's brother Robert came back nearly two weeks after they had initially arrived that Johnny agreed to train.

There was, however, a change in the structural dynamic of his team after the Johnson fight: Teresa became his manager. Close friend of the family and Johnny's agent, Bob Case, who Johnny endearingly called "Bopper," suggested it to Teresa soon a few months earlier. Case referred to many of the people in boxing as greenflies—people constantly trying to suck fighters dry of their finances. One day he said to Teresa, "Why don't you manage him. You're one of the smartest people I've ever met." Both Teresa and Johnny looked at him like he was nuts.

Before Teresa met Johnny, she was working for an insurance agency while attending a class at Parks Business College. With a passion for some form of government work, her intention was to become a Russian interpreter, which was topical at the time, with U.S. and Russian relations being somewhat fractured. Managing a fighter was a stark difference in vocation, especially when it came to Johnny.

Case continued to argue the point: "Manage him, then the money's in the family and nobody's trying to pick the gold out of your teeth. You'll do great." Teresa, one of few women involved in sports management at that time, would do a fantastic job in the shark-infested waters of boxing. She was his manager, his lover, his mother, his therapist, and his best friend. Without her, Johnny wouldn't have seen his thirtieth birthday.

Johnny's zest for the square ring hadn't wavered, and over the next eighteen months, it was business as usual. Although he had to apply for travel permits for any out-of-state bouts during this time, he defended his WBO world super-flyweight title seven times and fought in three more contests in between, simply because he wanted to fight.

Meanwhile, back home, someone had started to take over Johnny's limelight. There was only one thing to do: settle it in the ring.

Resurrection Boulevard

*"The [temptation] for greatness is the biggest
drug in the world."*
—Mike Tyson

Toward the end of 1996, a storm had started to build between Johnny and fellow Albuquerquean Danny Romero, who held the IBF world super-flyweight title. While Johnny was in exile in Big Bear, Danny had become the new kid on the block and was being portrayed by the media as New Mexico's clean-cut, stronger, younger, bigger, and harder-hitting golden boy. Johnny was apparently out of his depth against a 30-1 opponent who represented everything that he had thrown away in life. The sportsbooks agreed with the media and had Johnny down as a 3-1 underdog.

Danny used the media slipstream to his advantage and refused to fly on the same planes or share any space with Johnny, air or otherwise. This irritated Johnny. On April 30, 1997, a press conference was held for their fight and Johnny literally flew over the table Danny sat behind to get a piece of him. From that point on, the two had to have separate press conferences, separate weigh-ins, separate everything, simply because nobody could trust Johnny.

Says Teresa: "Johnny could be your best friend or your worst nightmare, and for Danny, he was now the second." It was as if the lion had reappeared from the bush to prove his rights in the pride, even if the training camp didn't reflect his hunger and desire.

Johnny went through over twenty trainers during his professional career, and this camp was a prime example of why. Hall of Famer Emanuel Steward was brought in as the principal trainer, but Johnny fired him on the first day because Steward sent over his assistant, which Johnny thought was disrespectful. Johnny then decided to go on a drug binge and was in and out of jail right up to three weeks before the fight.

Next up was Eddie Futch, a great mentor and strategist but, at eighty-six years of age, Futch couldn't get in the ring and hold the mitts. In the meantime, Johnny started sparring at the Top Rank gym. He always had three types of sparring partner: those who outweighed him by about twenty pounds, lighter ones who helped with speed, and those who fought exactly like Johnny's opponent. That was standard for Johnny's camps . . . when he attended them. He trained in Big Bear to benefit from the altitude, but he ended up hanging out in Vegas, which was well over one hundred degrees at the time.

When elite boxing matchmaker Bruce Trampler saw Johnny in camp, he pulled Teresa aside and said, "What the hell's wrong with him?" Johnny looked terrible, and everyone was getting the better of him in sparring, but Teresa declined to divulge the truth. Everyone was worried apart from Johnny, as he let the world know, "Danny's not going to beat me. He's going to have to kill me to beat me."

With just over a couple of weeks until fight night, Jesse Reid was brought on board, acting as the voice of reason and calm. Johnny had a special relationship with Reid. He respected the trainer's "no-bullshit" attitude, but also his lighthearted character. For example, Reid would turn up to training wearing a Hector Camacho shirt and Johnny would say something like, "Really? You're wearing that shirt today?"

Knowing the deep-rooted hatred between the fighters going into this bout, Reid advised Johnny, "One thing that could be your downfall is if you try to do power for power with Danny. He might get lucky and stop you. I wanna show them your boxing ability. Use your jab to win and get him frustrated, because I don't think he's ever been in a real chess match before. Once we get past five rounds of doing that, I'll turn you loose. You're a hell of a boxer. You don't need to try to kill everybody."

Hundreds of police officers were on duty at the Thomas & Mack Center in Las Vegas on July 18, 1997. With rival fans and gangs expressing their hatred for each other, metal detectors were enforced, more so for Johnny's supporters, who the police viewed as a genuine threat because of his gang involvement.

The fight was competitive, but Johnny was always in control, winning a comfortable unanimous decision. Soon after the fight, he gave his IBF championship belt to Bob Case as a gesture of friendship and gratitude. When Johnny grew up broke and barefooted, he used to go to Wells Park and wait until somebody walked in there to steal their shoes when they were playing basketball. When he had millions, he had a closet with hundreds of pairs of shoes; and if he liked you, he'd give you a pair. That was his way of saying he really liked you. He'd given Case about ten pairs over the years, because he was a close friend, always supported the family and never charged a dime for his services as his agent.

Case understood Johnny at a level many didn't. One day, they were asleep on a plane and Johnny woke up and said, "Bopper. Am I a bad guy?" Case woke up and said, "No. You're a good guy. You're just a product of your environment." Johnny replied, "Thanks Bopper," and went back to sleep. Case said many years later, "I can't think how many times I've thought about that since he's passed."

● ● ●

After two successful defenses of his IBF and WBO super-flyweight belts, Johnny needed surgery on his left rotator cuff, his money arm. He was supposed to be out for a whole year, but Johnny wasn't having any of it. Teresa and the doctors had to beg him not to fight while he was healing from surgery. The compromise in the end was to fight Carlos Francis Hernandez on August 29, 1998, just to test out his tools. Thankfully everything was in working order and on December 5, 1998, Johnny decided to move up in weight and challenge the WBA bantamweight champion, the tough Ghanaian Nana Konadu.

This, in simple terms, was not an easy fight. Sammy Stewart, who had fought Johnny in 1996 and who was living with Bob Case at the time, echoed those sentiments to Case: "Don't let Johnny fight Konadu. He knocks everybody out in sparring. Everybody."

Case, scared to death, said to Teresa, "We can't take this fight. It's too big a risk."

Johnny was famous for licking his blood off his gloves in fights, waving at the crowd and goading his opponents to punch him in the head, but that night he adopted a change of strategy. Because of his respect for Konadu, he left his showboating shoes at home and exchanged them for master-tactician boots. Shortly into the fight, Johnny tested Konadu's power and later said he heard bells as his punches landed. In fact, Johnny maintained that Konadu was the hardest hitter he faced in his career. Instead of standing and trading, Johnny boxed beautifully that night, working behind the jab, using angles, superior footwork, and speed to overcome Konadu and take a points victory to become a two-weight world champion.

Yet Johnny's work for the night was not yet complete. After the fight, as he was walking along the boardwalk in Atlantic City with Teresa, he gave $100 to a homeless man. At the time, Johnny was one of the highest-paid fighters in the lower weights—a seven-figure fighter. He hardly ever saw his paychecks, however—and that didn't bother him. Teresa was in charge of the finances, which bearing in mind his drug volatility was a wise move. As long as Teresa would allow him cash when he wanted something like a car, a watch, or some other luxury item, he was happy. He called that his fun money. They had a mutual account, but Teresa also gave him a separate account, which he hardly ever touched because he couldn't trust

Mr. T working Johnny Tapia's corner during
a fight versus Rafael Granillo at Olympic
Auditorium in Los Angeles on June 24, 1994.
Tapia won by technical knockout in round nine.
Holly Stein/Allsport

Tapia does his trademark backflip after defeating Ivan Alvarez to retain his WBO junior-bantamweight title at Caesars Palace in Las Vegas on June 7, 1996. *AP Photo*

Johnny and Mickey Rourke. In addition to other celebrities, such as William Forsythe and Sammy Hagar, Rourke worked Johnny's corner on occasion. *Courtesy of Teresa Tapia*

Johnny's friend and agent Bob Case with Mickey Rooney, whom Case also represented. Rooney loved Johnny and was a great source of support and wisdom. *Courtesy of Bob Case*

George Chuvalo, Johnny, and Bob Case ahead of a fight with Hugo Soto. Chuvalo, a longtime friend of Case's, was brought in to work Johnny's corner for the bout. Tapia won by unanimous decision and retained his WBO world super-flyweight title at the Sports Stadium in Albuquerque on August 17, 1996. *Courtesy of Bob Case*

Johnny and Manny Pacquiao. *Courtesy of Teresa Tapia*

Johnny and Mike Tyson had a special bond
because of the similarity of their backgrounds.
Courtesy of Teresa Tapia

WBO junior-bantamweight champion Johnny Tapia goes to the body of IBF champion and Albuquerque rival Danny Romero during their fight at the Thomas and Mack Center in Las Vegas on July 18, 1997. Tapia defeated Romero by unanimous decision to unify the titles. *AP Photo*

Johnny celebrates his victory over Danny Romero, which was the most satisfying of his career. *AP Photo*

Johnny Tapia throws a left at Nana Konadu. Tapia outboxed the dangerous Ghanaian to win the WBA world bantamweight title by majority decision on December 5, 1998, at the Convention Center in Atlantic City. *The Ring/Getty Images*

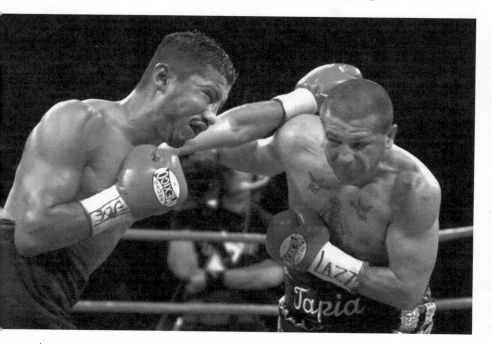

Johnny Tapia exchanges punches with WBA bantamweight champion Paulie Ayala during their fight at the MGM Grand Gardens in Las Vegas on October 7, 2000. Ayala was awarded a unanimous decision although most observers believed Johnny clearly won the fight. *John Gurzinski/AFP/Getty Images*

himself. He'd take out $500 at a time and give it out to homeless people. He'd also buy them meals and clothes. He loved doing that.

So here he was in Atlantic City doing what he loved outside of a boxing ring.

Shortly after giving the homeless man the money on the boardwalk, Johnny and Teresa heard a commotion, only to see that the same man was now being beaten up by a group of seven or eight people. Johnny darted off as Teresa shouted, "Leave him alone, leave him alone!" She was, of course, referring to the homeless man, as she had no doubt about her husband's ability to defend himself. Next thing the assailants started dropping like flies as Johnny let his hands go, while the rest ran off. Teresa recalls: "He didn't care if it was inside or outside of the ring, he needed to fight. He felt alive when he fought."

• • •

If Johnny Tapia had been raised in a different environment, he could have been a doctor or a lawyer. He was highly intelligent. Instead, his mother was murdered when he was a kid and he was surrounded by addicts growing up, some of whom put him in cockfights when he was just nine years old against kids as old as fifteen, so they could bet on him. It's no surprise that Johnny grew up to be a fighter.

Yet despite a difficult upbringing, Johnny's grandparents took him to all his boxing matches, made sure he had all the necessary equipment, and were his biggest fans. Without a doubt they were essential in helping the young Johnny reach his necessary stepping-stones as a successful amateur boxer.

Johnny never strayed far from the underground scene throughout his career as a professional, however. In fact, that is what he loved most. There were no rules, except you couldn't use a loaded gun. He'd been stabbed and hit with brass knuckles in what was a crazy world, but that never deterred him from returning.

Johnny had also been shot at a number of times. It was no secret that he was affiliated with the Wells Park gang. As opposed to many people's motives to become part of such a group, for Johnny it was more to do with being proud to represent and protect his local area. So much so that the community center in Wells Park is now called the Johnny Tapia Community Center.

On one occasion, Johnny was fighting in a park as part of the gang and the cops started to let loose with gunfire. The man Johnny was fighting was shot dead in the head right in front of him. To say Johnny's life on the streets was crazy would be an understatement.

Early into Johnny's professional boxing career, Ken and Frank Shamrock used to be part of his security detail. MMA had exploded on the scene as the ultimate no-holds-barred fighting discipline, and Johnny used to joke with them saying, "Man, if that would have been around when I was growing up, that would have been my perfect sport." It was never about money. Johnny would fight to defend people, he would fight because he felt disrespected, he would fight just to fight.

By the time Teresa met Johnny, he'd had his nose broken numerous times because of his street fighting. He used to knock on his nose and tell her, "This is a multimillion-dollar nose," referring to the purses his nose had earned him in the ring. After over twenty breakages and regular visits to the doctor, it got to the point where he would be in the dressing room after a fight and the doctor would say, "Your nose is broken," and Johnny would reply, "I know." Then he'd crunch it together and say, "It's set." His nose alongside his scars were almost a vest of valor. Physically, Johnny feared no man and no pain. The only thing that terrified him was losing Teresa and his kids.

• • •

By 1999, Johnny had re-signed with Top Rank for a two-fight deal, with the cherry on top being the matchup against southpaw Paulie Ayala, on

June 26, 1999, in his first pay-per-view headliner. An impressive first-round knockout of Alberto Martinez two months before Ayala was the perfect preview for the showdown against the Texan.

Johnny was going through a good patch. He'd been clean for several months and didn't have the media on his back. Unfortunately, there were a couple of time bombs ticking away in the background. First, Johnny turned thirty-two years old on February 13, 1999. Ever since his mother was murdered, no matter how much money he made or how many accolades he picked up in the ring, he lived continually with a huge void in his heart.

The moment he turned thirty-two, his depression ramped up a few notches, as he believed he was doing a great injustice to his mother by living beyond her number of years. He also blamed himself for her death. He would constantly tell Teresa, "I wish I'd done something, said something, reacted in a different way that night. If I'd have been stronger, she might still be alive."

Teresa recalls: "When Johnny turned thirty-two years of age, it was a race against time trying to keep him alive."

The other seismic eruption waiting to happen was also connected to his mother. Teresa had been in contact with their attorney regarding reopening the unsolved murder. If Johnny could find out who was responsible for his mother perishing, it would give him partial closure.

With the murder investigation taking place in the background, the Ayala training camp was running smoothly. Now trained by Freddie Roach, Johnny was preparing at high altitude in Ruidoso, New Mexico, and the atmosphere in the gym was fantastic. One day, less than three weeks until fight night, Johnny had run out of water at the gym, so Teresa ran to the store to get some.

Minutes after she left, the phone rang in the gym, and Johnny was the first to answer. It was the District Attorney's office, requesting to speak with Teresa. Johnny's gut instinct knew the call was something to do with his mother's murder, so he managed to charm the DA into sharing what he was going to tell his wife. The DA proceeded to tell Johnny that the murder case had been solved—an unfathomable high for Johnny.

Unfortunately, that glory lasted only a matter of seconds as the DA continued to explain that the killer would never face justice because he had been run over by a car and killed about ten years after murdering Johnny's mother. Teresa had been gone only fifteen minutes, and when she returned, she felt like she'd walked into the twilight zone.

Johnny fell instantly into a deep depression, refusing to train or eat. Void of sleep, he sat in a dark room not talking to anyone. The consensus of everyone involved with the Ayala fight was that it needed to be postponed. When this was communicated to Johnny, he became angry and said nothing or no one was going to stop him. His rationale was that the fight would allow him to release his rage. Without that, he was afraid of what his other options would be.

• • •

The mood in the dressing room was somber on fight night. As the fighters started to warm up, the police and the Las Vegas boxing commission swarmed Johnny's room, saying they would not put up with any shenanigans from him or his team. Already on tenterhooks, this put Johnny further on edge. "When we walked out of the dressing room to walk to the ring, it felt like Johnny was being led to his own hanging," Teresa recalls.

As well as escorting Johnny and his team to the ring, the police also had a huge presence inside the arena. This had happened only one other time and that was for the Romero fight, at the IBF champion's request. As soon as Johnny's name was announced, all hell broke loose. Johnny's grandfather, who was over eighty, was shoved by police, Johnny shoved Ayala, and Teresa's brother and brother-in-law were dragged out of the ring and cuffed. Teresa now had to jump in the corner to replace her brother. Not the ideal start to any fight.

Bob Case was ringside and, as the fight got underway, he would give Teresa a thumbs up or down for each round that was scored. Before the final verdict, Case, who was sitting close enough to the judges to have a feeling of the outcome, gave Teresa a thumbs down. Knowing that Johnny had suffered his first professional loss, rather than give anyone the satisfaction of seeing his reaction, she pulled him to the corner and informed him the way it might go.

As the official announcement came moments later, fights broke out through the arena. The contest was close, but many thought Johnny had done enough to secure the win. The police reported later that it was one of their rowdiest nights in the history of law enforcement at a boxing match.

After the fight, Johnny went into a very dark place. He didn't care about anything and notified Showtime of his retirement. Teresa was the only person who could get through to him, and even she was struggling this time. He disappeared for two and a half months, back to his drugs, back to that world. Teresa would hunt him down, get him home for a few weeks, and would nurse him back to health, then he'd disappear again. It became a soul-destroying cycle for her.

In the coming weeks after the fight, Johnny tried to kill himself on two occasions. The first time was in Nevada. He was holding a gun, getting ready to complete what he'd set out to do. Teresa walked in on him, ran over and lunged at him, forcing him to drop the gun. When the gun hit the floor, it went off, leaving a bullet hole in the wall. The second time was in New Mexico when Johnny stabbed himself with a steak knife. On both occasions, he was admitted to mental health facilities for about a week.

Shortly after being released from the facility, Johnny confirmed that he had bipolar disorder. One morning, just as everyone was walking on eggshells in front of a depressed Johnny, unsure of what he was going to do or say next, he jumped up and announced, "OK. I'm done. I'm coming out of retirement." He signed to fight Jorge Eliécer Julio on January 8, 2000, in Albuquerque, for his fourth world title.

Freddie Roach trained him for this one, and, despite Johnny's new-found confidence, both Freddie and Teresa's brother were concerned. They were looking for signs that Johnny was not focused and were getting ready to make excuses to the media just in case Johnny took off. Thankfully, Johnny acted as a model student during the camp. He did what needed to be done with Freddie to get himself fighting fit, both mentally and physically.

Julio boasted a record of 42-1 at the time and had stopped thirty-two of his opponents. The tough Colombian did not intend for Johnny to walk away with his WBO world bantamweight belt, but that's exactly what he did, with a wide unanimous-decision win. *Boxing News* in the UK praised Tapia's intrepid comeback. "With 90 seconds left, Tapia slammed home a triple right hand which brought a loud, disbelieving cheer. Ever the showman, he had closed this latest show in style."

Four months later, on May 5, 2000, Johnny defended his title against Pedro Javier Torres. Despite saying in the buildup, "I prepare for each fight like I'm training to box Mike Tyson and nothing's changed," the reality was that Torres came with a journeyman's record, and Johnny found it tough to rise to the occasion. He took the fight simply to fulfill his obligations to the promoter.

Johnny preferred to fight warriors like Romero or Konadu, and the Argentinian didn't come from the same mold. In addition, Johnny was busy with the Showtime series *Resurrection Boulevard*, where he played himself. For that to generate more interest from Johnny than his opponent tells you about his motivation level stepping into a boxing ring.

Thankfully, his next opponent could provide what he wanted, plus the opportunity for a little revenge.

Cheating Death

"He had talent and skills from the beginning and, as he gained ring experience, he became a better fighter. Big heart, advanced boxing smarts, great athlete, solid chin, decent punch, above-average hand speed, and terrific instincts. That he overcame so much drama and negativity outside the ring made him, to my way of thinking, even greater than his ring record shows. Talk about handicaps. It would be like putting a three-hundred-pound jockey atop a racehorse."
—Bruce Trampler

Five months later, on October 7, 2000, Johnny had the chance to settle the score against the only man to have put a blemish on his professional boxing record: Paulie Ayala.

At their first fight, Johnny had been battling the demons of his mother's murder investigation. A year and a half later, he'd come to terms with the fact that there was nothing he could do: The man who had killed his mother was dead, and Johnny had mentally worked through that process.

Comparatively, the training camp for the Ayala rematch was a lighthearted affair. Johnny's intention was to put on a show this time around, and that's exactly what he did. From the opening bell, he boxed beautifully behind his jab, following up with straight rights, hooks, and uppercuts—but he never cemented his feet, which prevented Ayala from gaining traction and making the fight a slugfest, as he had in the first fight.

Johnny then put on a boxing clinic in the middle rounds, working well off the back foot with a tight defense, as Ayala moved forward from his southpaw stance with clubbing shots, playing into Johnny's counters.

At the start of the tenth round, Jesse Reid, back as trainer, told Johnny, "Go out there and have fun," believing that his fighter was winning comfortably. By this stage, the consensus was that Ayala needed a knockout because Johnny had won between seven and nine of the rounds.

In the twelfth and final round, Ayala put his hands above his head as if to say, "I've won this," but the television commentator responded by saying, "The look on his face doesn't seem like he's won. He doesn't even look excited."

Unfortunately, despite the boxing media and a majority of fans world-wide believing Johnny had done more than enough to gain victory, the judges edged it to the Texan once again.

The television commentators spoke with disbelief when they said, "It's happened again! I just can't agree. I just don't understand that type of decision." *Boxing News* added, "Johnny Tapia was twice hospital-ized for depression and has contemplated suicide, but in Nevada they have their own idea of 'shock treatment.' Tapia just got robbed, after he fought superbly and appeared to beat Paulie Ayala in their exciting 12-round rematch."

Johnny's response on the night was perhaps less diplomatic, yet con-veyed the same sentiment: "I boxed his butt off."

• • •

The intention after Ayala was to either fight "Prince" Naseem Hamed or Erik Morales. Teresa had engaged in conversations with Naseem's brother and manager, Riath, and an agreement was in place. Johnny loved Naseem's presence and charisma in the ring, and it was a fight he was genuinely excited about. Said Johnny: "Put us two personalities together and it will be a special fight." Unfortunately, Naseem got beaten by Marco Antonio Barrera, which pulled the plug on the contest.

Another high-octane battle of wits and wiles that never came to fruition was against Manny Pacquiao. The evergreen Filipino fought Agapito Sánchez in November 2001, with Johnny supposedly fighting the winner. The result was a draw, and the fight with Johnny simply never materialized.

Instead, Johnny took on César Soto, a veteran of sixty-six fights, at the Mandalay Bay Resort in Las Vegas on June 30, 2001. The fight was seen as high risk by many because of Soto's natural size, durability, and one-punch power—he'd stopped forty of his opponents.

Consistent with his previous modus operandi, Johnny hired and fired a number of trainers during the training camp, but thankfully a few stuck around long enough to make an impact. George Chuvalo was brought in by Bob Case to assist, but it was Buddy McGirt who ended up taking over the principal reins.

While Teresa was genuinely concerned for her husband given the choice of opponent, McGirt allayed those fears. "Don't worry. He's the right fight for us."

"He's going to outweigh Johnny after the weigh-in by at least thirty pounds," Teresa commented.

Buddy replied with a relaxed manner and a smile on his face: "Don't worry! He's got to catch him in order to hurt him."

The strategy on fight night was simple: McGirt told Johnny to fight on the inside and go to the body of the former WBC featherweight world champion—don't get involved in a slugfest and keep a cool head in a hot kitchen. Round one went as planned, but in the second, Soto stepped on Johnny's foot, Johnny fell over, and referee Joe Cortez gave him the eight-count. Johnny got up and pushed Cortez, who knew he meant nothing by it and let him carry on without any penalties.

Johnny came out in the third round with a clear head and a left hook to the Mexican's liver, which rendered Soto unable to make the ten-count. This was the first time Soto had ever hit the canvas during his fifteen-year career.

Seven months later, Johnny made the trip across the pond to the UK's mecca of small-hall boxing—York Hall in London—to take on Eduardo Enrique Alvarez. The reception he received from the British fans was incredible. Tickets sold out within a matter of minutes of the fight being announced and, on the evening, hundreds waited outside hours in advance of the fight, just to grab a glimpse of their visiting hero. Richard Maynard, then head of press and publicity for Frank Warren Promotions, recalled, "We'd promoted Johnny for three fights—from the first Ayala match up to the Torres fight. The support and fan base he had out there was absolutely incredible. Around the same time, we also promoted Mike Tyson's first fight in the UK. Possibly two of the biggest personalities in boxing, but also maybe the most disturbed.

"I'd heard about his [Johnny's] dark side, but I never saw any of that. My memories of him were this tiny little thing who bounced up to you and gave you a big hug. When he came up to the office he said, 'Who wants a game of pennies?' Basically, you had to flick pennies against the wall and the one who landed closest to the wall won. Which Johnny did of course. He hustled us!"

Johnny's unpredictability and raw passion drew crowds. Maynard recalled the hours before the doors opened. "The queue. I've never seen anything like it, prior to that night or since. It started off at the front of the York Hall and stretched all the way past the back entrance. A lot of fans didn't have tickets and never made it in. Some just wanted a glimpse of Johnny."

• • •

Against Alvarez, the intention was to put on a show but to be cautious against the Argentinian who had challenged for the IBF world super-bantamweight title eighteen months earlier. Trainer Eddie Mustafa

Muhammad gave Johnny his instructions shortly before the bell went. "Let's start off with the jab, feel him out, and see what's up."

"OK, champ," Johnny replied.

The bell rang, Eddie walked down the stairs to assume his position in the corner, and about thirty seconds later Johnny had knocked out Alvarez with a body shot. So much for tentative tactics.

Before the count was over, Johnny performed his backflip to a standing ovation and thunderous round of applause, quickly followed by a walk around the ring and a shout of "London!" in appreciation of the warmth from the fans.

With the Alvarez fight firmly ingrained in British boxing folklore, Johnny set his eyes on winning another world title, in yet another weight class. The thirty-five-year-old had his work cut out for him against the IBF featherweight champion Manuel Medina on April 27, 2002, at Madison Square Garden, but once again, he rose to the occasion to overcome his 2-1 underdog status.

Different opponent, different trainer. Inevitable really. Jesse Reid, the man in charge for this fight, told Johnny: "Don't try to headhunt him. He's very awkward and he's very difficult to hit to the head."

Johnny prided himself on his durability. He was a big fan of the fifteen-round format and had the engine to go the distance. As Reid said, "He was one of the toughest, most determined athletes, but he could also box." Stamina, however, wasn't the issue. Johnny knew he was slowing down and couldn't capitalize on opportunities as quickly as he had in the past.

He went straight at Medina with his inside game and, despite Johnny landing multiple shots and throwing a high volume of punches, Medina exploited his weakness. He fought Johnny on the outside and used his superior reach to jab and run. Johnny got frustrated because he couldn't catch up with him and land the combinations he'd been practicing. Medina was the first opponent to do that to Johnny. It proved to be the beginning of his decline. Far from an easy fight, Johnny still walked away with a majority-decision victory.

Johnny was now a three-weight, five-time world champion. Yet despite his most recent achievements, the fight had also exposed his age and a visible slowing down in his capabilities as a fighter.

Undeterred by any decline in output or a step-up in opponents, in advance of his next fight against Marco Antonio Barrera on November 2, 2002, Johnny boldly expressed to the media: "I know I can go to the hospital to get fixed up if I get black eyes, broken ribs, and noses."

Johnny respected Barrera and looked at him as everything he wasn't. The Mexican never did drugs, was clean-cut, and had pursued a law degree, before dropping out in his third year of study at La Salle University in Mexico City in 2000 to concentrate on his boxing career. He used to say to Barrera, "Why would you want to fight? You're smart and have a good family." They also shared the same surname. Despite being known as Marco Antonio Barrera, Tapia was his last name and was always displayed on the back of his shorts.

The fight itself was one of the most courteous affairs, with both fighters touching gloves at the start of each round and neither taking any cheap shots. Johnny lost by a wide decision that night, but he didn't lose any love from his fans. Throughout the evening, everyone was shouting, "TA-PIA, TA-PIA," including Mike Tyson. Even after the press conference, Barrera admitted it was the first fight he'd attended where he couldn't hear any of his own fans.

After the fight, Johnny chose solace in drugs yet again. He headed for a mobile home in the middle of about three acres of land in a tiny town on the outskirts of Kingman, Arizona. With no neighbors, fans, media, or police in the vicinity, it had been his secret getaway on more than one occasion. Acquainted with Johnny's post-fight movements and always in fear of his overdosing, Teresa would often hire security people to follow him, just to make sure he was safe, although she ultimately couldn't stop him from taking drugs.

On this occasion, Johnny was doing drugs with one of his relatives who was on the run when bounty hunters caught up with them. Johnny being

Johnny, he didn't want his relative to be found guilty on any further counts, so he swallowed all the drugs they had without informing anybody. The bounty hunters let Johnny go on the condition that Teresa pick him up.

Later that evening, the inevitable happened: With the drugs now working their way into Johnny's bloodstream, he passed out. He had foam coming out of his mouth and his face had turned gray. It was not the first time Teresa had seen this, so she immediately called an ambulance, which took him to the University Medical Center in Nevada.

Within minutes of arriving, there was a media frenzy, which then generated the attention of every fan in New Mexico. Hundreds of people turned up to support Johnny both outside the hospital and at the Tapia residence, while various television channels were on-site, with helicopters hovering overhead. The presence of global superstars such as Mike Tyson, who had come to visit Johnny, probably didn't help, causing security more hoopla than they were used to experiencing.

If that wasn't enough, the calls to the hospital from well-wishers all around the world were in the thousands, and soon sent the switchboard into meltdown. It got so bad that the hospital had to create a dedicated phone line for Johnny. If you called the hospital, you'd get through to the automated service, which said, "Call 1 for . . . , 2 for . . . , and if you're calling for Johnny Tapia, dial this number." You'd then get through to another message that said, "Please don't come down to the hospital—his condition will be updated hourly."

With the amount Johnny had ingested, it should have been a fatal overdose, but instead he went into a coma. Freddie Roach was with Teresa at the hospital and called Bob Case.

"We don't think Johnny's going to make it," Roach told Case.

Case rushed from California to Las Vegas to say his goodbyes. On the trip over, he thought, "How am I going to handle saying goodbye to this kid?"

As he walked in, Johnny popped up wide awake and said, "Bopper! Can you get me a burger and fries?"

Johnny added to his comical script when Mike Tyson called him on hearing he'd regained consciousness. Tyson, genuinely concerned for his friend, mentioned he could recommend a good psychiatrist to help him. Johnny laughed and said, "You're giving me advice? I guess crazy knows crazy!"

A couple of days after Johnny was admitted into the hospital, Teresa sneaked him out. There was no way they could return home with the media having taken over their street, so instead they went to an Arizona hotel and casino, which Case's friend organized. Entering through side doors and service elevators, they called this their home for the next few days until things calmed down. Once Teresa saw a window of opportunity, she took Johnny to New Mexico until he was fit again.

Guilt Trip

"Life is a gamble. You can get hurt, but people die in plane crashes, lose their arms and legs in car accidents; people die every day. Same with fighters: some die, some get hurt, some go on. You just don't let yourself believe it will happen to you."
—Muhammad Ali

To an extent, the Barrera fight was the start of Johnny's long walk to the finish line as a boxer. He was aware that age was catching up with him, and he was trying to figure out his future. Letting go was a slow and gradual process, as boxing provided him with a precious lifeline.

From 2003 to 2007, Johnny fought only six times and not against any opponents of note. His life was still a whirlwind of family, drugs, and alcohol, but Johnny's sense of humor was always present. Then something happened in spring 2007, which was to trigger a downward spiral for him.

About three weeks after his fight against Evaristo Primero on February 23, 2007, Johnny and Teresa were due in court in Albuquerque to sort out an issue with back taxes. At the time, Johnny, Teresa, their kids, Teresa's mother, Teresa's brother and his wife, his children, as well as Johnny's godson and nephew, Benny Garcia (who was a Golden Gloves champion on the cusp of turning professional), were all living together in Farmington, New Mexico.

Everyone except Teresa's mother decided to make the trip to Albuquerque in support of Johnny, and they all stayed at the same hotel. The next day they went to court, did what they needed to, and then the following night Johnny disappeared and nobody could find him.

Teresa's mother was on dialysis in Farmington and someone had to be there with her, so Teresa's brother Robert made the decision and said, "I'll go back and be with mom. Let me know if something changes with Johnny." Benny joined him.

On the third night, there was finally a knock at the door, and Johnny walked in high as a kite. Although mad at him for disappearing, Teresa was relieved that he was back. Johnny retired to the bedroom, where he fell swiftly into a deep sleep. In the early hours, Teresa was awoken by their baby crying and went to give her a bottle. As she awoke, she checked on Johnny and noticed he had irregular breathing, and once again, foam coming out of his mouth.

Try as she may, she couldn't wake him. Minutes after Teresa dialed 911, asking for a paramedic, but without letting them know the person in question was Johnny Tapia. Johnny had always told her not to give his name over the phone, as that would alert the media. Somehow, having only asked for an ambulance, the police also arrived. Perhaps they recognized Teresa's number and figured it out.

Soon after the ambulance arrived, Johnny was being rushed in an ambulance to the hospital. The doctors didn't think he was going to make it and, if he did, there was a high probability of brain damage. Meanwhile, Teresa's brother was in Farmington, about two hundred miles away, and the media contacted him: "Give us a quote about Johnny."

Robert instantly called Teresa. "Johnny's dying? Why didn't you call?"

"He's in ICU at Presbyterian Hospital," Teresa replied. Robert jumped in the car with Benny to come back to see Johnny in Albuquerque.

Johnny woke up from his coma at around 3 a.m., in front of a room full of people. "That was weird. Robert and Benny were here last night," he said.

"No they weren't," Teresa replied.

"Yeah they were," Johnny insisted. "They wanted me to go with them, but I told them you'd get mad."

Teresa was unsure of whether she'd perhaps dozed off during their visit and called Robert's wife, Gina. "Johnny said he saw Robert and Benny last night." Both Gina and Teresa believed Johnny and started to look for them in Albuquerque.

Then, at about 11 a.m., Teresa's mother called, crying hysterically. "He's dead! He's dead!"

Teresa assumed she was talking about Johnny. "No. He's fine. He's woken up," she told her mother.

"Not Johnny," her mother replied. "Robert. Your brother."

On March 13, 2007, both Robert and Benny were pronounced dead in a car crash on the way to see Johnny. Robert was like a blood brother to Johnny, and the hardened world champion would never be the same. He knew that if he hadn't have been high that night, they would not have been in the car that morning.

The guilt consumed him until his dying days.

Hanging Up the Gloves

"I was always a big fan of Johnny Tapia from his early days and was honored to fight on his undercard. I never knew or witnessed the struggles he had outside of the ring but, like so many of us, he put on a very good face in public. Problem is, you never know what demons people are fighting behind closed doors."
—Christy Martin

The ramifications of Johnny's actions from the night he went to the hospital in March of 2007 continued beyond the death of his brother-in-law. When the paramedics and police were called to the scene that night, they took off Johnny's shorts and found a significant amount of cocaine on him. He was consequently charged with possession of narcotics.

Johnny went before a judge, who then placed him into a treatment facility instead of prison. The problem was, he was getting higher inside the facility than on the streets, so Teresa went to court to get him out, explaining he would without a doubt perish in there. Johnny was then placed on probation, on the stipulation that he have treatment in Las Cruces, New Mexico, where he lived at the time.

Turn the clock forward to 2008 and Johnny was still on probation, when one day Teresa left him a parting message while on the way out to taking their kids to school: "Johnny, you need to get ready and go see your probation officer."

"No problem," he replied, but by the time she got back, he was on the couch passing out. Despite Teresa's best efforts to wake him, Johnny's eyes were far from opening from his drug-induced nap.

She ended up calling his probation officer. "Johnny's under the weather," she told him. "Can we reschedule?"

After being informed that they were already on the way to her house, Teresa hung up and called her eldest brother, who lived a couple of blocks away.

"Can you help me get Johnny to the hospital before they find him?" Teresa asked him. Teresa's brother arrived, and, just as they were walking Johnny to the car, the probation officers turned up. They took one look at Johnny and said in a panic, "Get him to the hospital immediately!"

Teresa, her brother, and Johnny hopped in the car and headed for the hospital. As they drove down the road and came to a stop sign, Teresa noticed that familiar foam coming out of Johnny's mouth and a deathly coloration in his face. At that same moment, she spotted a police car behind them and flagged it down.

The second the officers saw the state of Johnny, they called an ambulance. When the paramedics arrived, they soon determined that Johnny's heart had stopped. They went to work on him for about fifteen minutes on the side of the road. Miraculously, his heart started to beat again, and he was rushed straight to ICU.

While the doctors were trying to figure out what he had overdosed on, Teresa received a call from her mother. "I think he got into my insulin," she said. "I found a needle broken in half with an empty bottle of insulin." It would transpire that he'd shot that whole bottle into his veins.

Despite this newfound knowledge, doctors were fearful Johnny wouldn't survive and had already warned Teresa that if he pulled through to expect brain damage. For the next two days Johnny was on a respirator, incapable of breathing independently.

After over forty hours, Johnny woke up. The first thing he did was look around and say with an air of relief, "I'm not in jail?"

When Teresa told him he was instead in the hospital, he laughed and said, "It worked!"

"What worked?" she replied.

"I knew I was dirty and had probation, so instead of giving them a urine sample and going to jail, I decided to overdose. It was a gamble, but if I survived it, I probably wouldn't have to go back to jail."

He who dares.

• • •

Johnny did eventually end up behind bars in 2009 for his various offenses relating to drug possession. He was given an eighteen-month sentence to serve in Los Lunas prison. He hated it from the moment he arrived because they kept him segregated from everyone else. He was desperate to be placed in general population, but they were worried he was going to hurt someone or they were going to hurt him. As a result, he was kept under lockdown for twenty-three and a half hours a day, sitting in his cell going crazy. He would only get out for fifteen minutes to take a shower and a further fifteen to walk in the dog-run area outside.

Johnny was an extremely sociable soul and couldn't handle the routine. He was constantly going back and forth to court pleading to be placed in general population and, finally, after ten months of lockdown, his wish was granted. Unlike what the authorities had assumed, he got along with the other prisoners, made people laugh, played basketball, and had a new lease on life, as he showed everyone he was just a regular guy.

With eight months still to serve, an opportunity for Johnny to be released early was presented. He would have to agree to commit to a certain number of hours of charity work, giving something back to the local community. The only thing he knew how to do was fight, so he said, "I'll fight three times and give the purses to charity."

Johnny therefore signed a three-fight contract while behind bars in early 2010, with the first of the trio being against Jorge Alberto Reyes on

March 6, 2010, followed by Jose Alonso on September 24 the same year. With his tools still sharp, he stopped them both in four rounds.

Johnny's last fight was set for June 4, 2011, in front of his home crowd at the Hard Rock in Albuquerque. However, this was more than just the last installment of the prison promise; it would be the last fight of his illustrious career.

Johnny's team wanted him to fight a soft touch and sign off with an easy celebration. Johnny picked Mauricio Pastrana.

Despite the Colombian's best fighting days being more than a decade behind him, coming off a string of losses and not carrying the same stamina he had back in the '90s, Tapia's doting wife nevertheless expressed her concerns. "He was a former world champion who campaigned at four different weights and is six years younger than you."

"You don't have faith in me?" Johnny replied, knowing the question had always bothered her.

"Of course I do," she answered.

"I don't go out fighting a nobody," Johnny continued. "That's who I'm fighting."

With a relentless crowd cheering him on, Johnny, now forty-four, fighting at a higher weight and with fire in his belly, won a wide decision to the delight of his adoring Albuquerque public.

• • •

Despite a happy ending in the ring, things behind the scenes weren't rosy. In 2009, his good friend and fellow fighter Arturo Gatti died in mysterious circumstances at the age of thirty-seven, but the loss that affected him more profoundly involved Diego Corrales, who passed away in a motorcyle accident in 2007, only two months after Teresa's brother had died.

Corrales was fighting César Morales on the same show as Johnny, who was top of the bill as he defended his WBO super-flyweight world title against Hugo Rafael Soto. His trainer, Willy Borchert, was in Arizona and wanted Corrales to train with Johnny. They got along so well that Corrales ended up living with Johnny and Teresa in Albuquerque for several months. It was during that time they became very close, with Johnny looking after Corrales like a protective big brother. When he heard about his passing, he cried profusely.

The day he was sentenced to prison was the same day Teresa's mother had passed away, just four weeks after Teresa's grandmother had died. It seemed like everybody dear in Johnny's life was being taken away, and the thought started to consume him. Being in lockdown in prison also messed with his head, giving him too much time to think. He was not the same Johnny when he came out, constantly in a hurry to do things, setting goals for himself, convinced he was running out of time.

When he got out of prison in 2010, Teresa had a gym already open for him in Albuquerque called Team Tapia Boxing Academy. When Johnny trained for his last few fights, the gym was supposed to be closed to the public; however, Johnny allowed people to come in. He liked to have people around. He'd see them on the speedbag or heavy bag and turn around and say, "No. Hit it like this. Hold your hands like that. Move your feet like this."

Being a trainer was a natural thing for Johnny to transition into, and he did it with passion. Unfortunately, he was telling everybody who would listen "my time is short," while in the same breath saying he wanted to reach the highest heights as a trainer just as he did as a boxer.

In the end, the first scenario would have a stronger hold over him.

Final Bell

"I looked at him every day and tried to memorize the lines on his face because there was a part of me that knew I wasn't going to have him for a very long time. Then there was that hopeful part of me that wanted to grow old with him and watch our kids and grandchildren get old. Unfortunately, what I soon learned was that I couldn't take him away from drugs, because he wasn't ready to be taken away from them and never would be."

—Teresa Tapia

E ver since Teresa's brother passed away in 2007, the family would go to his gravesite to celebrate his birthday on April 30. On this day in 2012, Johnny, for whatever reason, didn't go along.

Teresa and her sister had been to the gravesite and had taken a number of photos, one of which clearly showed her brother's face on his headstone. When Teresa showed Johnny the photos the day after, on May 1, that particular shot instantly grabbed his attention, giving him the chills.

He turned to Teresa and said, "That's who they sent for me? Robert G."

Teresa replied, a little confused, "What are you talking about?"

From that day forth, Johnny started planning his funeral. He told Teresa, "I want my funeral to be held in The Pit, the casket to be in a boxing ring, and I want a celebration, so people can talk about the good stuff."

"Why do you have to be so morbid?" Teresa replied, upset. "What is wrong with you?"

Yet Teresa was taking in every detail he uttered. A day didn't pass from then on when he wouldn't mention his funeral plans.

At the time, Teresa's sister and brother-in-law ran the Tapia Boxing Academy. On Wednesday, May 23, 2012, Teresa received a call from her sister, informing her that Johnny was throwing up behind the garbage cans there. Somebody earlier that day had visited the gym and given Johnny some form of narcotic, but nobody had any idea what it was.

For the next two days, because of Johnny's hallucinations, Teresa and her family were on twenty-four-hour watch, ensuring no harm came to him. By Friday he was coming off whatever he was on and had started to act like his usual self. One of their sons was eight at the time and had strep throat. He was in bed and Teresa had just given him a popsicle while Johnny was standing in front of the mirror.

All of a sudden he looked over at her and started crying.

"What's wrong?" Teresa asked.

"I'm going to miss you," he replied. "I love you so much, but I have to go."

"You're not going anywhere," she told him. "What are you talking about?"

"I love you and our boys, but it's time. It's time."

Later that day, Teresa found a letter that he'd written, telling her that he was sorry but that he knew he had no more chances left.

The next day, they celebrated their oldest son's twelfth birthday, but Johnny was uncharacteristically quiet. He told Teresa his stomach hurt and asked her to go get some medicine for it.

"Your stomach always hurts because you drink a twelve-pack of Dr. Pepper every day and eat gallons of ice cream!" Teresa replied. Either way, she went and bought him some Pepto-Bismol.

On the morning of Sunday, May 27, 2012, Teresa's sister came around to take her sons out to a movie. Teresa went up to Johnny's room and asked him to go see *Men in Black* with them.

Johnny makes his entrance at The Pit in Albuquerque before his fight against WBO bantamweight champion Jorge Eliécer Julio. He defeated the Colombian by unanimous decision to win his fourth world title. *AP Photo*

Johnny after defeating Eduardo Alvarez by first-round knockout in London on January 19, 2002. The English fans loved *Mi Vida Loca*. *John Gichigi/Getty Images*

Manuel Medina walks into a left hand from Johnny Tapia during their IBF featherweight championship fight at Madison Square Garden on April 27, 2002. Tapia won by majority decision, and loved fighting at the historic venue. *Al Bello/Getty Images*

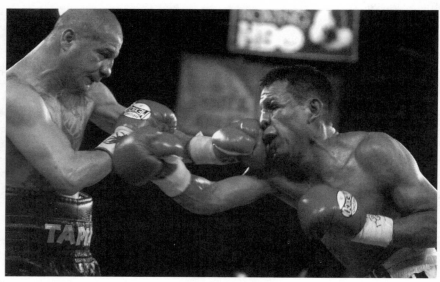

Johnny and Teresa Tapia share a moment together. *Courtesy of Teresa Tapia*

Johnny and Teresa after she was given an award for distinguished service by the World Boxing Hall of Fame. *Courtesy of Teresa Tapia*

Johnny and family friend Ray De La Cruz Jr. *Courtesy of Teresa Tapia*

Tapia with his brother-in-law and best friend Robert Gutierrez at Gutierrez's wedding. *Courtesy of Teresa Tapia*

Teresa at Johnny's memorial service at The Pit in
Albuquerque on June 3, 2012. Fans shared their
memories of Johnny during the service. *AP Photo*

Pallbearers position Johnny's casket in the boxing ring that was constructed for his memorial service. *AP Photo*

Dylan Vargas, who trained with Johnny, bows in front of the casket during Johnny's memorial service. *AP Photo*

Teresa and her sons, Johnny Tapia Jr. (L), and Johnny Tapia III, at Johnny's induction into the Nevada Boxing Hall of Fame at Caesars Palace in Las Vegas on August 8, 2015. *Steve Marcus/Getty Images*

Teresa gives a speech in honor of Johnny at his induction into the International Boxing Hall of Fame in Canasota, New York, on June 11, 2017.
AP Photo

"I don't want to. I'm tired," he replied (which Teresa said was the norm if you tried to get Johnny to do anything before midday).

Johnny urged Teresa, "Why don't you go? I'm going to sleep anyway."

"OK," she replied. There was nothing abnormal about this behavior; Teresa had seen it a thousand times before, but she had a weird feeling that morning that something was different.

As she backed out of the driveway with the kids, her sister, and live-in nanny Pam, Teresa said, "You know, we're the only house without an address. We don't have a number on the front."

As they drove away, Teresa's weird feeling got worse, so she asked her sister to stop at the Lowe's store. "I need a number for our address. What if there's an emergency?" She found what she was looking for and then they went to the movies, where Teresa couldn't sit still.

When her sister asked her what the matter was, Teresa replied: "Johnny usually calls every five minutes, but he hasn't called." She started calling him, but he wasn't answering.

Halfway through the movie, Teresa, overcome with emotion, announced that she wanted to go home immediately. The second she got back to the house, she rushed up the stairs and knocked on the bedroom door. There was no answer. She then opened the door, didn't see Johnny on the bed, and assumed he must have gone on a binge.

As she was pacing outside the bedroom door, trying to figure out where Johnny was, she turned on the hallway light. There was Johnny, laying on the floor, facedown wearing a pair of socks and basketball shorts. Teresa had witnessed Johnny DOA at hospitals on numerous occasions, but this time she knew something was different. The second she looked at him she burst into tears.

Teresa knelt down beside him, touching and kissing his cheek. He was still warm.

An emotional Teresa recounts: "I started saying to him, 'You better have not left me, Johnny. If you've left me, I'll hate you. This was supposed to be us together. Please get up, Johnny. Please. Just get up.'"

Teresa called 911 but realized she didn't have a number on the house, so they wouldn't know where to go. She went outside the house and waited in the middle of the street so the ambulance could see her. Minutes later, they pulled up and rushed to where Johnny was laying.

When they walked out, the paramedic told Teresa, "Ma'am, I'm sorry."

Unable to accept the news of the man who constantly defied death, Teresa replied, "We're talking about Johnny. He always comes back."

Alas, Johnny would not wake up this time. The official cause of death, as recorded on his certificate, was "complications of hypersensitive heart disease," with prescription drug ingestion being a contributing factor.

New Mexico's most decorated sportsman had twenty world-title fights and never lost a single contest in his hometown, but on May 27, 2012—the day before the thirty-seventh anniversary of his mother's death—the last round of Johnny's Tapia's tormented life came to a shattering close in Albuquerque. He was forty-five.

Adios Johnny

"It was the biggest funeral in the history of New Mexico. About 7,000 people attended and they turned away a few thousand. Unheard of. He lived 500 years in 45 years."
—Bob Case

Teresa's role as guardian never ceased, even when Johnny's heartbeat did. Whitney Houston had passed away three months earlier and Johnny was friends with her husband, Bobby Brown. Shortly after she passed, Bobby said how the media had sneaked in to take pictures of Whitney in her coffin and in her body bag. Johnny turned to Teresa and said, "Don't you ever let that happen to me. I want people to remember me as a champion. My immediate family can see me in my coffin, but nobody else."

All that was now coming back to Teresa, and despite the house being full of people and hundreds building up outside, she never allowed a single person to take a photo.

Teresa's focus was now on ensuring Johnny's funeral went exactly the way he wanted: as an honorable champion and loyal member of the community of New Mexico.

Teresa did a sterling job in following Johnny's requests. His closed casket was placed in the middle of the boxing ring in The Pit in Albuquerque, and she ensured that an abundance of his photos were on display, alongside his collection of championship belts. People lined up at dawn to attend the memorial, armed with candles, flowers, and homemade cards to pay their tribute. Unfortunately, around three thousand people were turned away, simply because of the number of staff who were being vastly outnumbered by the crowds. Some waited so long to get into The Pit that they needed to be escorted to the hospital to be treated for dehydration.

The outpouring of tributes was immense—from fans, politicians, and, of course, from the boxing fraternity. The likes of Paulie Ayala and Bruce Trampler were there, while many sent video messages to offer their condolences, including Marco Antonio Barrera, Mike Tyson, Oscar De La Hoya, Don King, and Freddie Roach. The number of videos sent from fighters all over the world was in the hundreds.

The following day, Pastor Richard Mansfield conducted a beautiful service at the New Beginnings Church in Albuquerque, where Johnny, Teresa, and their children regularly attended. "Johnny, you were always emptying yourself out to people with your love," the pastor said during the service. "Now you're getting that back."

Johnny's love for and loyalty to his beloved state never wavered. He would often be seen looking at the camera after a fight saying, "I love you 505." On that day, 505 (the area code for New Mexico) wept for their loss—and still does to this day.

Over the next few months, Teresa had Johnny's burial site constructed in the shape of a boxing ring—one of Johnny's wishes was to have his casket in the ring so that the mourners and admirers could pay their respects there. The grave was almost an extension of that in appearance and purpose. Since its construction, thousands of people from all around the world have made the crusade to Albuquerque to pay homage.

• • •

In the late 1990s, before his death, Johnny and Teresa made the pilgrimage to Canastota, New York, to witness the latest cohort of International Boxing Hall of Fame (IBHOF) inductees. This was certainly one of

Johnny's happier times, as he embraced the occasion and the setting where so many legends had previously walked on the ground he was standing on.

Johnny always had a deep-rooted belief that he would one day be inducted as a boxer, but he also wanted to be the first person to be entered twice, as a trainer too. His resumé tells you he was always going to be a candidate for the IBHOF, but also that he was never going to accept that award alive. Boxing gave him the discipline to do something other than put his life in jeopardy. When he retired, his family was concerned about what could take the place of his beloved boxing. The answer was, unfortunately, nothing. Nine months after the discipline of boxing left Johnny's life, so did his last breath.

Johnny Tapia was posthumously inducted into the IBHOF in 2017. Teresa accepted the award on his behalf, delivering a moving speech to those in attendance. Here was her conclusion: "Standing here before you all, I finally have an answer to Johnny's question that he sought in life. Johnny, you belong here in Canastota, New York, immortalized with all of boxing's greats, past and present. Welcome home Johnny!" Despite receiving a standing ovation, it was a bittersweet experience for Teresa, who desperately wished Johnny had been there in person.

A plaque featuring his photo and biography is on permanent display on the Hall of Fame wall, where fans can read about his career. Ed Brophy, IBHOF Executive Director, said in 2019, "Of the thousands of fighters who laced up the gloves, Johnny Tapia may have brought the most passion to the square ring. *Mi Vida Loca* fought with skill, intensity, and desire that elevated him to five world titles in three weight divisions and the love of boxing fans the world over."

Johnny's trophy cabinet could quantify his success in the ring, but how did he measure success in his lifetime?

"If I wake up, I know I'm a success. The day I don't wake up, I know I'll be home. I have one foot on this earth and one foot has crossed over. I didn't just die, I lived."

A big thanks goes to Bob Case, Jesse Reid, Clarence "Bones" Adams, Eddie Mustafa Muhammad, Pastor Richard Mansfield, Bruce Trampler, Sammy "The Red Rocker" Hagar, Christy Martin, and Ed Brophy. And to Richard Maynard for taking the time to add some anecdotal color to this book. Luca Rosi, thank you for your diligent editing.

Special mentions and RIPs to Johnny's surrogate father, Tom "Pops" Crego, and Earl Fash, VP at Showtime Boxing, who was always supportive of the Tapia family, even after Johnny's untimely passing.

Last but not least, a very special thank you goes to Teresa Tapia for opening her heart and shining a bright torch into a few of Johnny's darker corners, sharing some of his more uplifting moments, but, more than anything, for being the incredible lady that she is.

ABOUT THE AUTHOR

Paul Zanon has written eight books, with almost all of them reaching the number-one best-selling spot in their respective categories on Amazon. He has cohosted boxing shows on talkSPORT and has been a pundit on London Live and BoxNation. He is a regular contributor to *Boxing Monthly* and a number of other publications. Paul is a member of the British Boxing Writers' Club.

The Ghost of Johnny Tapia is set in 9.5-point Palatino, which was designed by Hermann Zapf and released initially in 1949 by the Stempel foundry and later by other companies, most notably the Mergenthaler Linotype Company. Named after the sixteenth-century Italian master of calligraphy Giovanni Battista Palatino, Palatino is based on the humanist typefaces of the Italian Renaissance and reflects Zapf's expertise as a calligrapher. Copyeditor for this project was Shannon LeMay-Finn. The book was designed by Brad Norr Design, Minneapolis, Minnesota, and typeset by Toppan Best-set Premedia Limited. Printed and manufactured by Maple Press on acid-free paper.

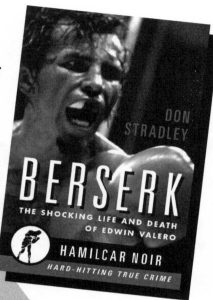

ALSO READ

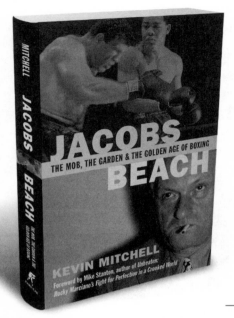

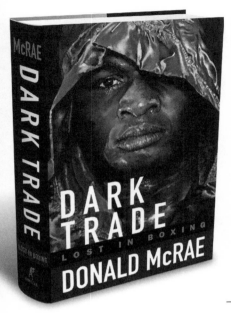

McRae brings to the highly charged, obsessive world of professional boxing a novelist's eye and ear for revealing detail and convincingly recalled dialogue. This is an impassioned book.

—Joyce Carol Oates, *Los Angeles Times*

When I started covering boxing in 1996, one of the first books I read to educate myself about the sport was Dark Trade—*and, to this day, Donald McRae's book has stayed with me. No collection of boxing books is complete without* Dark Trade.

—Steve Kim, ESPN.com

Over twenty years ago, Donald McRae set out across the United States and his adopted home, Britain, to find deeper meaning in the brutal trade that had transfixed him since he was a young man. The result is a stunning chronicle that captures not only McRae's compelling personal journey through the world of professional prizefighting, but also the stories of some of its biggest names—James Toney, Mike Tyson, Evander Holyfield, Oscar De La Hoya, Naseem Hamed, and others.

Singular in his ability to uncover the emotional forces that drive men to get into the ring, McRae brilliantly exposes the hopes and fears and obsessions of these legendary fighters, while revealing some of his own along the way. What he shares with them most, he comes to realize, is that he is hopelessly, and willingly, "lost in boxing."

In this new edition, released in the United States for the first time, and including a new chapter, it's clearer than ever why *Dark Trade* is considered one of the finest boxing books ever written.

Find *Dark Trade* at your favorite bookstore or online retailer! Or order online at www.darktradebook.com.

HAMILCAR
PUBLICATIONS
Boston

ISBN 9781949590050 | HARDCOVER | FEBRUARY 2019

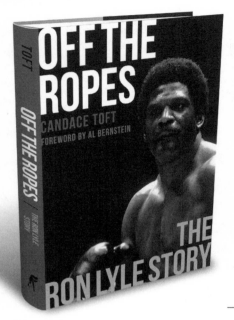

In her deeply researched biography of Denver's rugged contender, Candace Toft shows that Lyle's battles inside the ring, though dramatic, were mere shadows compared with the harrowing but ultimately redemptive journey of his life. Off the Ropes *is a reminder that boxers, like the rest of us, have to keep fighting, even when the bright lights have gone down and the crowds gone home.*

—Paul Beston, author of
The Boxing Kings: When American Heavyweights Ruled the Ring

O*ff the Ropes: The Ron Lyle Story* explores not only the greatest era of heavyweights in boxing history, but also tells an equally compelling personal tale. Ron Lyle grew up in the Denver projects, one of nineteen children in a tight-knit, religious family. At twenty, he was convicted for a disputed gang killing and served seven and a half years at the Colorado State Penitentiary at Cañon City, where he learned to box before he was paroled in 1969.

After a meteoric amateur career, he turned pro in 1971, and over the next seven years established an outstanding professional record, which, in addition to near misses versus Muhammad Ali and George Foreman, included a brutal knockout win over one of the era's most feared fighters, big-punching Earnie Shavers.

Then, in 1978, Lyle was indicted for murder a second time and, even though he was acquitted, his career was effectively over. The years that followed were filled with struggle, a captivating love story, and eventual redemption.

Off the Ropes: The Ron Lyle Story is the poignant, uplifting biography of a singular man.

Find *Off the Ropes* at your favorite bookstore or online retailer! Or order online at www.offtheropesbook.com.

9781949590012 | HARDCOVER | OCTOBER 2018

HAMILCAR
PUBLICATIONS
BOSTON